Pets

Teaching Tips

Red Level 2

This book focuses on the phoneme **/ss/**.

Before Reading

- Discuss the title. Ask readers what they think the book will be about.
- Sound out the words on page 3 together.

Read the Book

- Ask readers to use a finger to follow along with each word as it is read.
- Encourage readers to break down unfamiliar words into units of sound. Then, ask them to string the sounds together to create the words.
- Urge readers to point out when the focused phonics phoneme appears in the text.

After Reading

- Encourage children to reread the book independently or with a friend.
- Guide readers through the phonics exercises at the end of the book.

5357 Penn Avenue South
Minneapolis, MN 55419
www.jumplibrary.com

Decodables by Jump! are published by Jump! Library.

Library of Congress Cataloging-in-Publication Data is available at www.loc.gov or upon request from the publisher.

ISBN: 979-8-88524-712-2 (hardcover)
ISBN: 979-8-88524-713-9 (paperback)
ISBN: 979-8-88524-714-6 (ebook)

Photo Credits
Images are courtesy of Shutterstock.com. With thanks to Getty Images, Thinkstock Photo and iStockphoto. Cover - Eric Isselee, PetlinDmitry, mangpor2004, effective stock photos. 4 – Victoria Faladiy. 5 – anetapics. 6–7 – Sergey Novikov. 8 – uzhursky. 9 – Namning. 10 – Marina Fistina. 11 – Ksenia Raykova. 15 – Shutterstock.

Can you find these words in the book?

fuss

hiss

mess

It is Ness. Ness is a pet.

Ness can hop a lot!

It is Bess. Bess is fun.

Bess can hiss a lot!

It is Tim. Tim is a cat.

Tim can fuss.

It is Kim. Kim is a dog.

No! It is a big mess!

Can you say this sound and draw it with your finger?

Can you say this word and draw it with your finger?

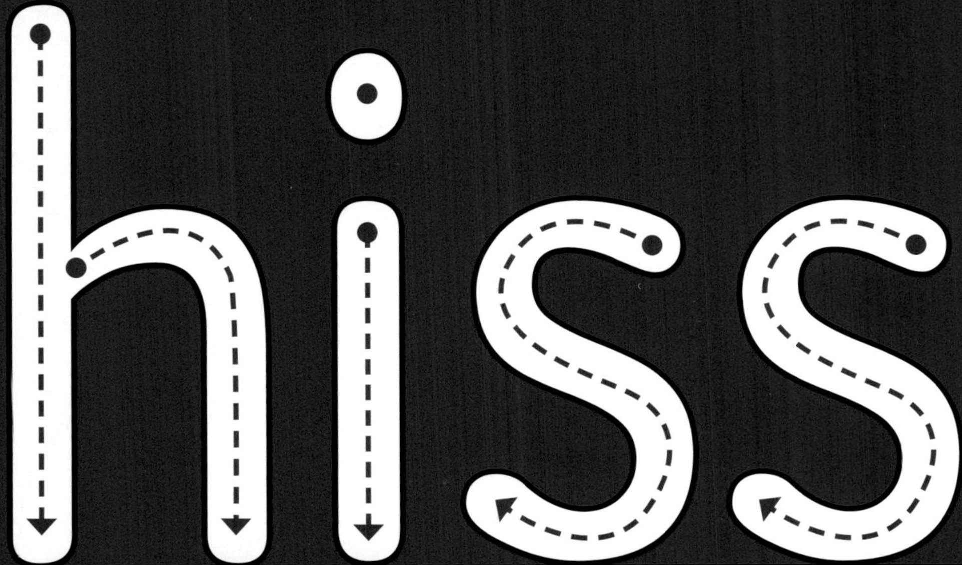

Using the Letter Bank, trace the missing letter into each word.

__et

his__

__ess

Letter Bank

m s p

What other words do you know with the letters /ss/?

kiss

dress

grass

Practice reading the book again:

It is Ness. Ness is a pet.
Ness can hop a lot!
It is Bess. Bess is fun.
Bess can hiss a lot!
It is Tim. Tim is a cat.
Tim can fuss.
It is Kim. Kim is a dog.
No! It is a big mess!